Today Is a Baptism Day

Today Is a Baptism Day

Anna V. Ostenso Moore
Illustrations by Peter Krueger

CHURCH
PUBLISHING
INCORPORATED

Church Publishing
19 East 34th Street
New York, NY 10016
www.churchpublishing.org

Cover art by Peter Krueger
Cover design by Beth Oberholtzer

A record of this book is available from the Library of Congress.

ISBN-13: 978-1-64065-099-2 (hardcover)
ISBN-13: 978-1-64065-100-5 (ebook)

To my family,
especially my parents and sister
and my love, David, who said,
"Of course that's a good idea."
—Anna

To all Godly Play students:
past, present, and future.
—Peter

Presented to

_____

From

_____

On the occasion of

_____

Date

_____

Today is a day of hope.

Hope in God's call to each of us as beloved children.

Today is a day of unity.

Unity in one God, one Faith, one Baptism.

Today is a day of love.

The love of your parents sharing the love of God with you.

Today is a day of community.

A community that will worship
and wonder with you.

A community that will nudge
you toward God.

Today is a day when we say,
"I will, with God's help."

I will learn, eat, and pray with others.

I will turn back to God when I've turned away.

I will share my stories and our Christian stories in what I do and say.

I will look for and name the Holy in everyone I meet.

I will respect every living being.

I will do all this with God's help.

Today is a day of Sacred Stories.

Sacred Stories that connect us to our Jewish relatives, to the people in our Bible, to all the followers of Jesus yesterday, today, and tomorrow.

Today is a day of water.

Water that gives and sustains life. Water that binds us to Jesus' life, death, resurrection, and ascension.

Water that you can feel and taste,
a sign of an inward grace.

Water that washes over you in baptism.

Today is a day of oil and light.

Oil, called Chrism, to bind you to the Holy Spirit.

Jesus' light to remind us that God is with us.

God is here.

Today is a baptism day.

A day forever after.

Family Pages

My Baptism Day

Tell your story. Add photos, draw a picture, and/or use words to describe your baptism.

My name is:

I was born on:

I was baptized on:

I was baptized at:

I was baptized by:

My parents are:

My godparents are:

My story:

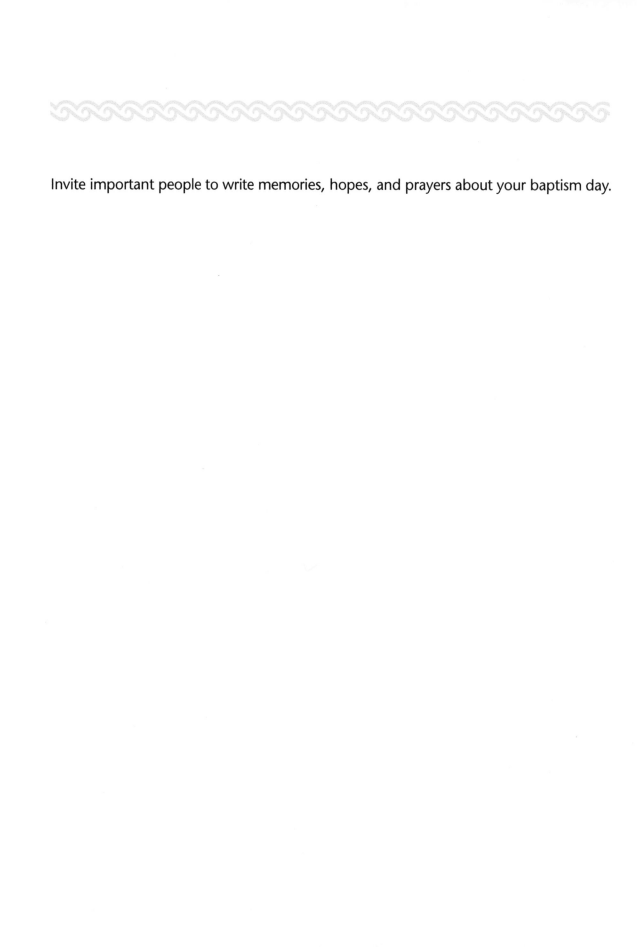

Invite important people to write memories, hopes, and prayers about your baptism day.

A Note from the Author

Baptism is a day forever after, because it is the moment when we, or our parents, say "yes" to the living God, and that yes invites and inspires transformation. We say yes to a God that adopts us as God's children and enfolds us into the community of believers who follow Jesus, a community often called "the Church," "the Body of Christ," or "Christians."

We say yes to learning and loving the sacred stories of Jesus and the Hebrew and Christian Scriptures. They become *our* stories to guide our lives and join the sacred stories of our faith community, our family, and ourselves. We will share all of them in word and action.

We say yes to the water that washes over us in the name of the triune God, a sign that we are united to the life, death, resurrection, and ascension of Jesus and that we are forever accompanied by the Holy Spirit.

We say yes that, although there are many different Christian faith communities, as Christians we all share in and are joined together by the ritual of baptism.

And although we say yes, we acknowledge that it is by God's grace, which often is a Holy Mystery, that we receive this gift. We call this gift of baptism a sacrament: an outward and visible sign of an inward and spiritual grace.

If you were baptized as a baby, your parents and godparents said yes. They promised to raise you within a church and to teach you about Jesus and how to follow him. Baptism as an infant is a gift our parents give us like the gift of our birth.

This book was written out of a hope to provide a tool for families to explore what saying yes to baptism means for them and how it inspires their lives.

On the following pages, I suggest ways to tell your family baptism stories and to remember those stories with rituals. These suggestions are meant as starting points to be adapted and personalized. Children have a concept of God and a sense of the Holy that changes as they age. Adults need to respect their experiences while helping them find vocabulary and practices to sense, name, question, and wonder about God. One of the best places to start is at home with our own sacred stories.

With peace from my family to yours,
Anna V. Ostenso Moore

Suggested Family Rituals and Spiritual Practices

Share Your Baptism Stories

This ritual is not just limited to children's baptisms. Share the story of each member of the family. Where was it? Who was there? What did you feel? What were your hopes? How has your life changed because of that day?

Show pictures and other memorabilia like service bulletins, christening gowns, or baptism certificates, cards, and gifts.

Read Other Sacred Stories

Together, look up in the Bible some of the sacred stories that inspired this book's illustrations:

Jesus' birth	Luke 1–2; Matthew 1–2:15
Jesus' baptism	Luke 1–2; Matthew 1–2:15
Miriam dancing	Exodus 15:20–21
Sarah laughing	Genesis 18:1–15
The Samaritan woman at the well	John 4:1–42

Find the illustration in this book that accompanies the biblical story you are listening to or reading. With a playful spirit wonder about it together as a family. Wonder what part is most important to you. Wonder what stories you would include. Wonder about the differences of answers. Do not assess each other's answers as right or wrong. Instead hold up each response as holy.

Baptism Anniversaries

Put the dates of everyone's baptism in your family calendar as you would birthdays. Create a way to celebrate them every year. Possible celebrations could include any of the story-sharing suggestions above. Light a baptismal or special candle. Pray baptismal prayers from the service or other sources. Offer a special blessing to the celebrant from each family member.

If you are not in the same place as the person celebrating a baptism anniversary, send a card or letter or call them.

Visit Other Churches and Faith Communities

When visiting other churches, look for their baptismal font(s). Notice the similarities and differences from the font where you were baptized. Where are the fonts located? Are they visible? What do they look like? What symbols are on them? Ask one of the church's members about the font(s). If there is water, touch it.

For additional resources and to share your baptism practices, visit www.annavostensomoore.com.